In Search of the Wild Dulcimer

poems by

Lana Austin

Finishing Line Press
Georgetown, Kentucky

In Search of the
Wild Dulcimer

ACKNOWLEDGMENTS

I offer immense thanks to the following publications in which my work
originally appeared:

Appalachian Heritage: "The Great Flood" and "The Pig"
Columbia: A Journal of Literature and Art: "Sex At The Ryman," "In Search
Of The Wild Dulcimer," and "Blood Harmony"
Mid-American Review: "Walking The Manassas Battlefield"
Southern Women's Review: "Doxology"
Switchback: "Greasy" and "Naming What Isn't"
The New Guard: "Scrambled Eggs"
Visions International: "Preserved"
Zone 3: "Bill Monroe Begat," "Beautiful Boy," and "The Future Woman"

Editor: Christen Kincaid

Cover Art: Lana K. W. Austin and Kent Ippolito

Author Photo: Thomas F. Austin

Cover Design: Elizabeth Maines

Printed in the USA on acid-free paper.
Order online: www.finishinglinepress.com
also available on amazon.com

Author inquiries and mail orders:
Finishing Line Press
P. O. Box 1626
Georgetown, Kentucky 40324
U. S. A.

Table of Contents

This book is dedicated to Tom, Alexandra, Michael, Kate-Elizabeth & Thomas.

I also offer gargantuan gratitude to my writing mentors, without whom this collection wouldn't exist: Claudia Emerson, Jennifer Atkinson, Eric Pankey, Jeanne Larsen, and Steve Scafidi. I also thank Betty Adcock, William Wright, Adam Vines, Jesse Graves, Danielle Deulen, Brian Brodeur, Kiley Cogis Brodeur, Peter Klappert, Richard Bausch, Katherine Soniat, Sara Henning, Kent Ippolito, Steve Watkins, Christian Teresi, Melanie McCabe, Annie Noble, Valerie Lambros Coughanor, Alycia Tessean, Sarah Colona, Katie Clare, Chris Tanseer, Shawn Flanagan, Amy Marshall Lambrecht, The Shelleys, my Hollins sisters, Kirsten Porter, Maria Maroon, Pamela Donnelly, Carolyn Wells & my Todd County teachers, Dr. Beazley & my Ars Nova family, Charlotte Baldwin, the Whites & Austins & my KY, VA, & AL family & friends. Soli Deo Gloria.

Sex at the Ryman

Yes, sex at the Ryman,
       but not quite what you think.

No, we didn't actually do it—
       my husband and me there

for our fifteenth anniversary
       to soak in the almost Patsy Cline

voice of Neko Case—but it made us
       (well, how should I put this politely?)

want to fuck, because even after
       fifteen years there's passion,

thank you God for this
       Song of Solomon seduction

still throbbing and you know it
       had to cross our minds to do the deed

'cause you know Patsy
       did it with her husband

or lovely Loretta with Doo,
       those salt of the earth sensual singers,

and if not there then maybe
       nearby in the alley

next to Tootsie's, at least some
       quick groping between sets

and dear heavens, I pray my preacher
        doesn't denounce me for writing

this, but I think he'll understand
        since every time he stomps up

in that pulpit there's as much wild
        physical force as fire and brimstone

and, please Grandma, don't roll
        in your grave after this, but I know

you won't since you had to
        have done it, too, and hard,

with my Grandfather, everything
        needing to come undone

in that fierce coupling, forgetting
        the crops that failed, the babies

you buried, clutching each other against
        the seasons turning, but not in that

moment, not in the savage union
        which held on to the here and now.

In Search of the Wild Dulcimer

I need something pure
with both a newborn

and dying woman's cry,
each connected to a single

line of light, one
at its beginning and another

at its end. Or is it more
of a curving river or a circle

of sound, unadulterated tremolo:
the dulcimer. I've found

Jean Ritchie, her ballad
matching her wild mountain

instrument, the one she made
by hand, the one born out of her

Scots-Irish Kentucky roots,
a simple incandescent strand

I somehow still hear
without much effort,

despite my rising deafness,
her voice and dulcimer

a single aural finger that points
to me. It grows both lonesome

and tremblingly full,
a rain cloud about to pour out

a host of voices from sky
to ground and back again.

Blood Harmony

A single larynx halved,
that's how I perceived it

when I sang with my half
brother—same mother,

long gone. She is
where it came from,

our ability to blend,
unique notes in a chord,

but still one voice. His tenor
a ginger effervescence,

and my aubergine alto
painting what felt like

caverns-deep undertones
in heavier hues,

our voices fused. Even
in measures when one grew

more dominant on lead
and the other receded,

growing hybrid harmony,
counterpoint shifting,

we were rivulets divined
from a vast river.

Creek, brook or stream—
water from the same source.

Greasy

Aretha, who needs no last name,
    called their playing greasy. Not
        something slithering

across a skillet, but the very
    fluid of life. Slick, sensuous, love-
        making wetness. Primordially

pure rhythm, a pulse, a new
    song from a bunch of white boys
        born by the Tennessee River

where Bono says, "The music
    comes out of the mud," and people
        like Paul Simon called producer

Al Bell, asking him, "Hey, man, I want
    those same black players
        that played on 'I'll Take You There.'"

Bell, who wrote the 1972
    Staple Singers hit, replied,
        "That can happen, except these guys

are mighty pale." So the mighty pale
    Swampers—Barry, David, Roger
        and Jimmy—played greasy and grew

the Muscle Shoals sound along with Rick Hall, that
    Crazy-like-a-fox white producer in Alabama.
        Rick and the Swampers created

their own little Melting Pot in a sound
        booth—not black, not white, but greasy,
                color-blind and throbbing and they all came

to sing with them, not just Aretha,
        but Percy Sledge, Etta James, the Stones,
                Arthur Alexander, Wilson Pickett and on and

on with the list of greats
        growing almost as long
                as the story of music, of life, itself.

Amulet of Sound

for Ricky Skaggs

Your hands become hummingbirds
flitting into a blur as your body shelters
not just a mandolin, but an amulet of sound.
Your fingers usher me through aural catacombs—

resplendent caverns of song—that defy dark,
until I have forgotten that my mother has forgotten
how to sing, her memory now immured,
her drunk tongue entombed.

Preserved

Don't worry if you bruise the fruit,
my mother said, when you're cutting off

the tops and chopping the rest up—the brown
fleshy parts make the sweetest preserves.

Move your fingers quickly, like your father's
combine, separating and harvesting

the crop—make your fingers the machine
and after a while they'll do it on their own—

like the muscle memory the organist
at church says lets her fingers play

"How Great Thou Art" without thinking.
And while I'd never been able to do two things

at once before, I'd waited long enough
to learn this trick of turning bitter fruit

into jeweled jars of sugar-thickened jam,
a process that left a smell in the house so rich

you felt the air around you might drop
to the ground, heavy. I'd also waited to learn

what the special ingredient was—the secret
all my grandmothers, aunts and older sisters

had kept like monogrammed handkerchiefs
saved a whole generation for a new bride.

Now everything was joining, an arc
of constant movement between my two hands,

the knife, the fruit, the bowl— the rhythm
I'd anticipated for so long, a song whose cadence

meant I was a woman now, old enough
to preserve things using knives and hot paraffin

to seal it all in. It took half an hour to notice
I'd cut myself, but when I told my mother,

as I started to throw out the ruined fruit,
she laid one juice-slickened hand on mine

to stop me, holding my finger up. That's deep
enough, she said, without going down

to the bone, to make this year's batch the best yet.
She told me to keep on working

as the bubbling water, ready to melt the wax,
was the only sound.

Bury Me in the Barn

When I die, bury me
in the barn. And if I die
young, please put me in
the tube top and Daisy Duke
short-shorts my mother forbade
when I was fifteen, saying
I'd look like a hussy. But, Mama,
I was a good girl and it
was the debutantes, no offense
to any of you reading this—
bless your little hearts—
who were the hussies. So,
dress me in that tube top
and some time between one
and three in the morning
I will rise up out of the dirt
and fly, all tarted up, to the top
of the rafters where the big owl
roosts and we will dance
around in the air and hoot
until the sun comes up
one last time before my body
hums again its dust refrain.

Warren County Grotto

Something smelled different.
 What his nose sensed was too thick,
  too round to be the lost cow he hunted,
  even if it was dead, since in his mind—
which sojourned for miles while his hands
performed their dirt rites
  on the same few acres—he saw
  the death smell as a long, thin line.
This was a different dark,
 almost a circle, as if
  he smelled an eclipsed moon.
And there it opened—
unfettered by the rain and mud
  that rolled stones and debris down
   a slight hill—a cave exposed.
He curled his head
and limbs into his center
  to enter through the small,
   storm-made door
  where he would later swear
he heard a subtle hum.
 The cave breathed,
  he would insist. He switched
 on the small flashlight
he always carried and saw
  it didn't grow spiky stalactites
   or stalagmites like nearby Mammoth,
  but he knew these caves were kin—
this was the top of a family tree
  that would later branch out
   into a maze of intricate paths.
 He saw gentle undulations

in the stone, many colors folding
on top of one another.
In the back the space tapered
to an unreachable point, so he turned off
the light and just listened
to a song deeper
than the earth's core.

Luthier
for Guy Clark

With cambered shoulders,
    his body in harmony
        with the arched surface he carves,
          the luthier summons
    the wood's spirit—a specter curving through
      a spruce or maple river—in the grain,
an eidolon in visual rhythm. Sometimes he
        stains the instrument a loamy brown
      with walnut husks or maybe he transforms
its color, varnished beyond just a luster
      into a shimmering.

But there are times
    when he transfigures it in reverse
    to the color of pitch
      with a dye brewed in a vat
of vinegar and nails, and it's then
      the luthier—more mid-wife
than instrument maker—births a paradox,
    a damned salvation of sound.

Canticle

Even as I bled out
with doctors and nurses panicking,
you blazed,
your vermilion skin glistening new
and the something more
hovering around you,
from you, so luminescent
it transformed
from glimmer to hum, a hymn
everyone hushed to hear.

Coffee and Blues

Around nine I got restless.
There wasn't a full moon,
just this hole in my stomach
for coffee and blues.

I walked to the place with no
name. A sign hung crooked
said, "Harmonicas Welcome."
I sat to the side in a green chair,

wobbly legs jerking at first.
The waitress came, I said black.
She knew, leaving me to stare
at a slinky woman, one spotlight

shooting right through her.
I don't remember much,
just all those dust pieces
standing still in the air

not daring to drop
to the floor until the last
saxophone note drew a fine line
and the woman moved

her mouth away. I wanted to
run up, see if she'd kissed
the microphone, caressing it
with those lips ready to spill

wicked wet onto themselves.
Instead I swished coffee grounds,
left a dollar and walked out a door
that squeaked when it swung shut.

Doxology

The sparrow seems more
than a sparrow today
with its gossamer warble crescendoing

to a coronet trill gleaming straight to my center
and the oak tree dazzles as matador,
flourishing its burnished copper and claret cape

and the spiced cider you brewed
in that old cast iron kettle melts luxuriously
on my tongue like manna and the Patsy Cline song

on the radio really does make me want
to go out walking after midnight where I can hear
those night blooms still whispering even now

and where the wood smoke smells of memory,
smells of my children's honeyed first days,
a startling thought that bursts out my finger tips as light

and there's a single firefly that doesn't seem to know
it shouldn't still be in the backyard
and my three year old says, "I think that bug

might stay with us forever." Yes, that one
firefly might just go on
with its magic trick glint forever.

Bill Monroe Begat

With a blessing from his itinerant fiddler
        Uncle Pen, and the blood harmony
            where he and Charlie—two
        high and lonesome hawks—
meshed the way only voices of kin can,
        William Smith Monroe
            and his Blue Grass Boys merged
        Scottish bagpipe, Folk, Gospel
and Southern Blues, speeding
            them up with a hard-drivin'
        mandolin for "Mule Skinner Blues,"
"Blue Moon of Kentucky,"
        "Uncle Pen," and "Raw Hide,"
            sometimes dancing like an Irish tinker,
and all the while his Kentucky
        gentleman's riding hat never moved.
            Oh, Father of Bluegrass, you begat

the Delmore Brothers, those mama's boys
        who took their mother's
            Gospel harmonies and put them in a jar
        with quicksilver Folk
and a dash of Blues
        until they shook it all up
        into the gin and whiskey
new country they poured out
            every night on stage until
        their rare tenor acoustic guitar, borrowed
            from antic Vaudeville, and that Delta
        choke-style harmonica had to give way
to the sexy electric guitar and drums,
        and hillbilly Boogie Woogie
        with "Barnyard Boogie"

and "Freight Train Boogie"—a new Country
Music that begat

the Louvins, with Ira's tenor flying
in a straight line of light
and Charlie's strawberry preserves melody
on ditties like "The Get Acquainted Waltz."
Even when the Grand Ole Opry told them
"you can't sell tobacco with gospel music,"
they clung to the mandolin—despite making
their electric guitar squeal—
to save them like a Healing Balm of Gilead;
they refused to go too Rockabilly,
and those tones begat

the Everly Brothers—Muhlenberg County's
golden sons, two more
Kentucky brothers blending
as only blood can—embodied the spirit
of everyone before them. You can hear ghosts
in "All I Have To Do Is Dream"
and "Bye Bye Love," songs haunted
by the faintest shimmer of Scottish ballads,
the relentless pulse of Blues
from Africa, and those dazzling
Gospel harmonies so close
they make the ears dizzy trying
to pick out one part as it folds over
and into the other, music unlike
any before. They topped the charts in Pop,
Country and R & B, with the bang and rattle
of the new Rock-N-Roll,
so the Everly Brothers begat

the Beatles, who could have been brothers
with their harmonies melding
into one glorious hum and we loved them
in America, yeah, yeah, yeah,
embracing their British moptop invasion
when they sang "I Want to Hold Your Hand"
and "Yesterday," somehow still bearing the mark—
like a similar smile passed down
generation to generation —the imprint
of our own original song,
that witch's brew of music
where Scotland meets England meets Africa meets
America, where we will pass on
something still larval
in the fecund soil of sound
whose origin is every place. Amen and Amen.

Highland Elegy

Deirdre McIntosh Shaw used her breasts
to come to America as a wet nurse, feeding
a rich woman's baby along with her surviving
son, Boyd, his twin sister and father flu-dead.

At first, while the babies suckled, she sang
Scottish ballads—metered stories draped
with melody—tall-tales of heroics and lewd
songs with bawdy humor. There, too,

came anguished refrains. Then she delicately
breathed out her lullabies, lilting phrases
in a subtle cadence to not disturb the infants, but
in her head she still heard sinewy bagpipes,

all tendon and screeching birds mourning
their fallen nests and her memory clung
to the Celtic flute's pure tone, a thin line
of lamentation. Soon, though, she stopped singing

to listen to the babies' lips and tongues stir over her
skin, draining her milk in rhythm while she remembered:
shadowed beats, the grief of dirges, bar songs
with the thump of beer glasses on tavern tables and those

Gaelic hymns' spherical resounding
in small chapels. And sometimes she fell asleep
with the children, mouth half open,
as if a song could still spill out.

A finalist for the 2015 James Wright Poetry Award, Lana Austin's writing has recently been featured in *Mid-American Review*, *The Writer's Chronicle*, *Columbia: A Journal of Literature and Art*, *Appalachian Heritage*, *Zone 3*, *Switchback*, *Southern Women's Review* and *The New Guard*. Also a journalist, she has written for numerous newspapers and magazines. Austin has received writing awards from Hollins University, The University of Mary Washington and American University. She studied creative writing at Hollins University and The University of Mary Washington as well as at George Mason University, where she received her MFA in 2008. Born and raised in Kentucky, Austin has lived in England and Italy but currently resides in Huntsville, Alabama with her husband and children. An adjunct instructor, she teaches multiple writing and acting courses and has also directed multiple theatre productions through Ars Nova.

CPSIA information can be obtained
at www.ICGtesting.com
Printed in the USA
LVOW04s0307200716

497040LV00018B/126/P